A CONFESSION OF FAITH

A CONFESSION OF FAITH

WILLIAM LILLIE

THE SAINT ANDREW PRESS
EDINBURGH

First published in 1974 by
THE SAINT ANDREW PRESS
121 George Street, Edinburgh

© William Lillie 1974

ISBN: 978-0-7152-0265-4

Printed in Great Britain by
Howie & Seath Ltd., Edinburgh

CONTENTS

		Page
	Prologue	vii
1	Natural Religion	1
2	Belief and Certainty	8
3	The God of Revelation	15
4	Ecce Homo	22
5	Christ Died for Our Sins	29
6	The Lord is Risen	35
7	The Holy Spirit	42
8	The Church of Christ	48
9	Christian Living and Christian Loving	56
10	Prospice!	64
	Epilogue	70

To

Adam and Anna

Prologue

When a man whose work in life has been chiefly the teaching of Christian truth has reached the threescore years and ten which Scripture regards as the normal life span, it is fitting that he should ask himself how much of his Christian belief has stood the test of life's experience. I imagine that most believers find, like myself, that some aspects of the Christian faith, which at one time seemed tremendously significant, are no longer of any real importance to us, and that in other directions there has been an increasing enrichment of belief with a growing sense of relevance. Of course, as well as gaining fresh insights, one has developed personal prejudices, of which there are probably too many in this book.

This is not an autobiography, although from time to time I shall mention some of my own experiences to illustrate or to justify the points that I am making. Nor is it a textbook of theology; there will be scarcely any direct references to scholarly works, and what of theology is in it will be what has grown in my own mind unsystematically and almost casually in response to the theological reading I have done. Nor is it intended to be a pattern, to be followed or avoided by others, of the Christian life, for one of the convictions which has grown stronger and stronger in my mind is that there are many very different roads by which Christians are led to him who is the way, the truth and the life. At best it may be of some comfort to others who share some of my doubts and hesitations. It is, as the title indicates, a confession, not in the sense that confession is an acknowledgment of one's own sinfulness (although I might well engage in such an exercise), nor in the sense that a confession is a formulary of the doctrines regarded by a particular denomination as essential. It is rather a personal statement of what I believe, and, although theologians have sometimes forgotten it, belief or faith is a very personal matter. To the critical mind what I write must seem an odd mixture of personal opinion and biblical truth.

Yet it would be wrong to claim any real originality for most of this book. Much of it I have learned from others, probably most of all from my own father who proclaimed the good news of Christ to a small country congregation with a directness and clarity that made no exhibition of the thorough scholarship which lay behind these preaching graces. And, again and again, while reading all sorts of writers from Dorothy Sayers to Katherine Mansfield, from Ignatius to Karl Barth, I have had the experience of a kind of illumination which makes me say, 'I know this to be true—true to my own experience as well as to the Christian tradition—although I myself could never have put it into words, and indeed I have never seen it put into words until I read this passage.'

It is not easy to be completely honest in such a confession of faith. There is a reticence about life's deepest experiences which is altogether seemly, and there is something peculiarly distasteful about spiritual exhibitionism. There will always be the temptation to state what I think I ought to believe rather than what I actually do believe. If I am led badly astray by that temptation I shall deserve the condemnation that our Lord pronounced on the Pharisees; they were hypocrites or play-actors. To claim absolute honesty for all that I write would be tantamount to claiming a personal integrity which unfortunately I do not possess. I can only ask that my readers, remembering this, regard my assertions with some sense of humour, and, as the saying goes, take my statements with a grain of salt. I hope that they may be sometimes salty in another sense, displaying the flavour of life's rich variety, and even at times salted more sharply by the fire of experience, of which our Lord once spoke (Mark 9: 49, 50).

CHAPTER ONE

Natural Religion

When a boy of eight or nine, while coming home from school, I was walking in schoolboy fashion in the almost dry ditch and not on the farm road, and I remember vividly, at a spot I could identify to this day, asking myself the question, 'Who made God?' I suppose that in school and Sunday school I had been told repeatedly that everything had been made by God, and, if being made was so universal a characteristic of things, surely God also must have been made in some way or other. I must have wisely decided that it was no use putting this question to anybody, and that, for a time at any rate, I had just to accept the fact that somehow or other God came into existence in a way nobody could explain. My question, 'Who made God?' was of course a very crude one, but it still seems to me in a very unsophisticated way to raise the issues debated but never solved by natural theology—the theology that depends on man's natural capacities and not on a revelation from God.

Behind my question there was the assumption that, as Lucretius said long ago, 'Nothing can be created out of nothing', or, as it was put in the elementary textbooks of inductive logic, 'Every event has a cause'. Of course philosophers express this assumption in a much more sophisticated and carefully qualified way today, but it is still an assumption at the back of most of our ordinary human ways of thinking, and, what concerns us here, it is an assumption behind the traditional arguments for the existence of God. There must be a first *cause* of all the happenings in the universe (the cosmological argument), or a designer who planned the complex structures of the universe with their inter-relations of *cause and effect* (the teleological argument), or an adequate *cause* of the idea of God (the ontological argument).

Once again I am putting things far too simply, but it seems to me that, in however learned a form scholars put these arguments, they all ultimately boil down to the view that what we know to exist, whether in the world of nature or in the mind of man, entails the existence of a being that men have called God. And all fail to convince because they all contravene the sound methodological principle known to philosophers as Ockham's razor, that we must not assume the existence of things when it is not necessary to do so. To take as an example the argument from design, in many ways the most appealing of the traditional arguments, it is no wonder that men are filled with wonder, love and praise when they contemplate the way that the forces of nature work together, like a perfectly designed piece of clockwork according to Paley and Butler. Yet this is no sound reason for inferring the existence of something still more marvellous—an omniscient and omnipotent God. To apply this to another argument, if something was created out of nothing, it is easier to believe that the amoeba rather than God came out of nothing. At best the hypothesis of God as designer and creator is one possible explanation of the apparent design and harmony of the universe, and it may add a rich content to the thoughts of those who have come to know God through revelation. As an American scholar has recently written 'It is doubtful whether natural theology has ever functioned significantly except for those already persuaded by faith.'[1]

The aim of any such hypothesis must be, as the Greek philosophers said, 'to save the appearances', or, as we in the modern world would say, to account for the observed facts. It needs a good deal of theological ingenuity (and theologians have never been lacking in such), to explain, for example, how earthquakes fit into the scheme of a universe designed by an

---

[1] D. B. Harned: *Faith and Virtue* (Saint Andrew Press, 1973), p. 11.

all-knowing and all-powerful God. They look dangerously like flaws in the design, and this is certainly how we would explain similar misadventures in a human construct like an ocean liner.

Of course philosophers and theologians have maintained for a long time, and most persuasively since Kant, that this whole concept of causation is at best applicable only within the world that is studied in natural science, either in the physical sciences or more recently in the human sciences like psychology and sociology. Many theologians, however, seem to me to have introduced this idea, sometimes in a disguised form, into their arguments about God, and it may be that the human mind is such as to be incapable of thinking without bringing it in. What I am maintaining is that from a purely philosophical point of view the existence of God can never be proved, and indeed, while it is a possible explanatory hypothesis it is in some respects not a very satisfactory one. While the arguments of natural theology may appeal to others with clearer minds and deeper sensitivities, my own experience has been very much that of Fitzgerald's Omar Khayyam,

> 'Myself when young did eagerly frequent
> Doctor and Saint, and heard great Argument
> About it and about: but evermore
> Came out by the same Door as in I went.'

Critics may rightly point out that up to now I have been writing about natural theology and not natural religion as the title of my chapter indicated. In natural religion, as contrasted with natural theology, we are not dealing with the abstract arguments of philosophical theory, but with the religious experience of the human race. Men, they say, naturally aspire after God, and their hearts are restless until they find rest in him. It is commonly held that men's other natural aspirations, for example towards truth and beauty, do imply the reality of the objects of these aspirations. Yet we must be careful here.

The fact that men are naturally superstitious, if it be a fact, does not prove that their superstitions are true, and many humanists would maintain that superstition and religion are closely akin. And, indeed, it may be doubted whether the majority of men are really religious. Once men get rid of the superstitious fears that, according to many thinkers, 'first in the world made gods', they are apt to get rid of religion altogether. We used to be told how much more spiritually minded the people of India were than we in the materialistic West. That may be true of a minority, but in my experience the European bank-manager is often as religiously minded as his Indian counterpart—the Hindu or Pathan money-lender. It is likely that in most countries the genuinely religious are in a minority, and that the prevailing practice of religion, so far as it does prevail, is due to the inspiration and leadership of people, whom we may loosely call prophets, who certainly have not obtained their religious beliefs from natural instinct or reason, but from something we call revelation.

We live in an age when many things that were formerly regarded as the business of religion have passed out of its sphere; this is probably what people mean when they say that man has come of age. Outwardly in our own country we have seen the education of the young, the care of the poor, and many kinds of social service pass from the control of the church to the generally more efficient control of the state. Again things that have been given a fairly adequate explanation by the natural sciences no longer require the religious explanation formerly given for them. A great deal of writing on ethics in recent years suggests that the time has come for morality to stand on its own legs apart from religion, although I myself do not accept this. The inevitable outcome of all this is that men think, quite wrongly in my opinion, that religion is limited to the practice of rituals, the speculations of theology and the cultivation of mystical experiences. All of these are outside the interests, if not beyond the capacities, of most normal human beings. The Bible shows the healthy-minded man's distrust of ritualism, theological speculation and mystic experience. The prophets denounced the sacrifices and other ritual practices of the religion of their time as useless and often offensive to God. Jesus thanked God that the truth which matters is hidden from the wise and prudent, and revealed to theological babes. Paul made it clear that various mystical experiences, even those which he himself enjoyed, are of very secondary importance. These things do have a great attraction for many of us, according to our varied temperaments, and there is no harm in them so long as we keep them in their place, and do not mistake them for true religion. But if these constitute the whole of religion or the heart of religion, we might be wise to follow the example of the Russians and relegate religion to the care of the state department that looks after museums.

One of the misconceptions to which loose thinking about natural religion has led is the popular view that there is a basic religious faith which is common to men of all religions, for it is the product of something within human nature as such. I have already expressed my doubt about the universality of religious experience, but it may be that there is something in man which can respond to the influences of revealed religion, although it looks as if this response can be negative as well as positive. More importantly if there be any natural religion in human nature as such it is what we might call the lowest common denominator of religion and not worth very much. I am not talking here about revealed religion, and as will be seen later, I would not deny that God has spoken outside the Judaeo-Christian tradition to which I belong.

Another weakness in much popular thinking today is the assumption that religion—any religion—is necessarily a good thing. It can be argued that in the course of history so-called religion has done more harm than good, and humanists put up a strong case for this view. I am not talking only of 'the heathen in their blindness' but of such things in the history of Christianity as have been in part responsible for the present tragedies in Ulster. When people say that religion is a good thing, they commonly mean that it is useful for social welfare and the like, but the important thing to ask about religious beliefs is not whether they are useful but whether they are true. The terrors of hell were probably a useful means of teaching for securing reasonably moral behaviour among ignorant and superstitious people; they are clearly of very little use for that purpose in the Western world today. Of course the real question here is whether the terrors of hell represent, admittedly in emotive and figurative language, something that is really true about the constitution of the universe. About that we shall need to think later.

This question of natural religion has become a live issue today, when many people in Britain wish to replace definitely Christian instruction in schools by a religious instruction that would be equally acceptable to children and parents of any religion. If what I have argued in this chapter is correct, such teaching would have very little positive content and would give a very poor impression of any of the world's greatest religions. Those who advocate this change use two other arguments, also fallacious in my opinion. They say that the indoctrination of children is morally wrong, and if they mean by indoctrination some methods of teaching that have been used in the past I am inclined to agree with them. But, if they mean that the children should not be led to discover that certain things are true, I disagree. Parents would take a poor view of a teaching of arithmetic that left the children in doubt as to whether two and two make four or five, and it seems much more important to me that children should come to know that God showed his love to all men in Jesus Christ than that their simple addition should be correct. Again we are told that it is the business of the teacher of religion to give an understanding of religion, but not to teach the practice of religion. I wonder what a teacher of music (perhaps the discipline in schools nearest to religion) would say, if he were told that his business was to give the children an understanding of music, but never to teach them to sing a song or play an instrument.

What seems to be needed in Britain today is not woolly talk about open-ended religion that leads nowhere but a firm decision as to whether the teaching of the Christian faith, making full use of our new understandings of child psychology and new educational methods, should still be the normal practice in schools. By and large parents seem to wish this, and teachers do not. If the present situation continues, and if there are larger numbers of children of other religions than Christianity in schools, there is much to be said for religious bodies seeking permission to bring their own teachers into day schools to instruct pupils of their own tradition. It seems increasingly likely that in a modern society the Church will have to assume the responsibility given to it by Christ for the Christian education of its children, the lambs of John 21: 16, and that will mean the transfer of much of its energies from a pastoral to an educational, or, dare I say, a missionary task.

CHAPTER TWO

Belief and Certainty

I suppose that every preacher is convinced that what he is saying in the pulpit is 'the truth, the whole truth and nothing but the truth', but the intelligent layman, and sometimes even the stray cleric, in the pew, without doubting the preacher's honesty, feels less and less sure of what he hears. As a generation we are unwilling to accept any statement simply because someone in authority says it, or because it is found in print! Some of us have probably gone too far and do not give due weight to the words of those who speak with real authority because of their knowledge and experience of the subject of which they are talking.

I used to tell my students a story about a conversation which I may have made up myself or borrowed from someone else. A sceptic, faced with the first words of the Creed, 'I believe in God', retorts, 'Believe in God? I don't believe in anything that I cannot see for myself. Your own Bible says that no one has ever seen God, and until I see God for myself, I am not going to believe in him.' This man, perhaps ignoring ambiguities in the verb 'see', declares that he does not believe in anything he cannot see for himself, but I wonder what he would think if I said to him, 'You know your wife doesn't love you.' If he does not knock me down for saying such an outrageous thing, he may well answer, 'Of course my wife loves me; we have loved one another for years.' 'Oh no,' I answer, 'you don't believe in a thing you cannot see for yourself, and love is something one cannot see.' 'Well,' he admits, 'I may not be able to see love itself, but I can see plenty of signs of my wife's love—all the things she does for me, the way she looks at me, the loving words she says to me—these are the proofs of her love.' If it is still safe to do so, I may reasonably answer, 'You remember the film star we saw in the Odeon last week. She showed all the signs of love to the hero, and she certainly knew how to show them, but in that story she really hated the man, and I hear that in real life she dislikes very much the actor who played the hero's part. No, my friend, you cannot be certain that your wife loves you. Only she knows what goes on in her heart, and she has you just guessing.' My friend, who, by this time, I hope, realises that he has lost the argument, says abruptly, 'You can say what you like, but I *know* that my wife loves me.' He is probably right of course, but if he is to be consistent, he must not go about saying that he does not believe in anything which he cannot see for himself.

This imaginary conversation illustrates certain things that I have learned about beliefs, and especially religious beliefs. When my friend said that there were plenty of signs of his wife's love, I might have pointed out the signs of the reality of God found in the created universe after the fashion of the traditional proofs, but I have already given my reasons for distrusting these proofs except as happy confirmations of what we know already. The more important thing that my friend has shown me is that it is possible for a man to believe with his whole heart something for which there is no direct evidence or logical proof. One of the very first real lessons I had in philosophy was from a little book by Bertrand Russell. When I say, 'I see a brown square table in front of me,' I certainly believe it, but actually that is not what I am seeing at all. It is not the table I am seeing, but an image mediated through chemical and other changes in the retina of the eye and the brain. This image is actually of an unequally sided quadrilateral and not of a square, and it is not of a brown surface but one with reflected lights that are almost white. Yet in spite of this, I still believe that the table in front of me is square and brown, but I cannot demonstrate this logically.

Again many scientists today would admit that what are popularly called the 'laws of nature' are not the absolutely certain truths that many ordinary people still imagine them to be, but statements of very great probability, extremely useful for practical purposes, but liable to require modification when new discoveries are made. Apart from pure mathematics and logic, and in my ignorance I have some doubts about these, we have to be content in life with reasonable probabilities. I accept the view of Hume and the logical positivists that propositions concerning empirical matters of fact are hypotheses, which can be probable but never certain. If the Christian religion is to some extent based on empirical matters of fact that were observed in the first century, then we are so far at least dealing with probabilities. Theologians who have realised this, and have disliked the discovery, have sometimes in the fashion of Spinoza tried to create a theological system by reasoning analogous to that used in mathematics, but their attempts have been generally unconvincing.

People used to say in my youth that the study of philosophy led students to agnosticism or atheism, and, in spite of the witness of thoroughly Christian philosophers, there is just a grain of truth in the common opinion. One cannot read Hume or Ayer without realising that much that has been said about the certainty of Christian beliefs is dangerously near to non-sense. What is wrong in the arguments of many unbelievers is that they so often demand that a Christian should give proofs for his beliefs of a kind that it would be quite impossible to give in any other sphere of human experience. What in turn is wrong with many preachers and theologians is that they attempt to give proofs of this impossible kind. This was the kind of proof that my friend in the story wanted before he would believe in God, when he would have been wiser to be content with the same kind of assurance as he had of his wife's love.

There is much confusion between certainty as a logical characteristic of statements and certainty as a psychological state of conviction. There may be people whose convictions are entirely determined by logical arguments, but I guess that they are few, and I certainly am not one of them. I am prepared to admit, as I shall in a later chapter, that many of my beliefs came to me to begin with from others, but what is rather vaguely called intuition has played a part. There was, I believe, a sense in which my friend did see or know directly his wife's love; it was more than seeing his percepts and concepts in a different pattern, as some of the psychologists would suggest. While I can claim no mystical visions or prophetic messages direct from God, I have in some of life's experiences known with a conviction of certainty the action of God. Sometimes while reading a book or listening to a sermon, I have apprehended a statement as true, although a logical study of it would reduce its certainty to reasonable probability. I might put this in another way by saying that commitment, the practical outcome of conviction, is more important than logical proof in the sphere of religion. It has often been said that conversion demands a leap of faith, presumably a leap over intellectual barriers. This certainly does not mean our accepting what reason shows by all reasonable probabilities to be untrue. It rather means accepting from a number of alternatives the one that not only seems reasonable but that grips in a strange way our whole personality, and betting our life on that. This does not apply only to dramatic conversions, but to a great many of the decisions we have to make throughout life.

Faith is for Christians not only intellectual acceptance but reliance on a person or putting our trust in him. This is what is expressed by our English idiom 'to believe *in*', which occurs in the creeds, and possibly by a corresponding Greek idiom found in the New Testament, particularly in John. When a person said during World War II, as many did, 'I believe in Winston

Churchill,' his intention was not to make a statement about his own psychological condition—a virtuous attitude of his own mind. He was saying that Winston Churchill was completely reliable and trustworthy. Similarly to believe in God is to find reliability and faithfulness in God, and to this the whole Bible bears witness. But faith is not merely the intellectual recognition of that trustworthiness; it is an act of commitment. It is possible for a man so to commit himself to God in Christ without an intellectual assent to every article of the creeds. Yet Christians hold that it is to God as he is in imperfect human language described by the creeds that they commit themselves in faith; we do need to believe that certain statements about God are true before we can put our trust in him.

Theologians like scientists use hypotheses, which the Oxford English Dictionary defines as 'provisional suppositions which account for known facts, and serve as starting-points for further investigations by which they may be proved or disproved.' In my experience theologians and particularly biblical scholars are sometimes careless in their treatment of hypotheses, although Shakesperian scholars seem to be even worse offenders. If they are challenged they admit that their theories are hypotheses, but often they go on to speak of them as if they were established truths, while even after full investigation they can only be regarded as reasonable probabilities. For example, New Testament scholars have made the hypothesis that the common material in Matthew and Luke, other than that found in Mark is taken from an earlier undiscovered document which they call Q. Much scholarly investigation goes to confirm this hypothesis, but it is still an hypothesis, and no scholar has the right to speak of it as if it were an established fact; there are competent scholars who do not accept this hypothesis. The preacher of a past generation was able to present his own hypotheses to his congregation, and so long as he could confirm them by sometimes arbitrarily selected Scripture texts, the man in the pew felt bound to accept them as gospel. This is not the case today and rightly so.

What worries many thinking people today is the nature of the language that theologians and preachers use. Much of it is obviously metaphorical or figurative language, and when this is said, many people assume that it is not what they call true, or true only in a very unusual sense. For example, all Christians usually speak of Jesus as the son of God, but Jesus was not the son of God in the ordinary sense in which we speak of a man being the son of his human father. Moslems think that this is what we Christians mean and despise us for holding such an unseemly belief about God. Should we then abandon this hallowed expression? In certain circumstances, for example in preaching to Moslems, the answer is probably, 'Yes.' On the other hand many of us believe that the relationship of God to Christ is a pattern or norm on which every human relationship of father to son is or should be modelled. It is, as it were, the Platonic idea of fatherhood, more real and perfect than any human fatherhood. Some thought like this may underlie Paul's statement that God is the father, 'from whom every family in heaven and on earth is named.'

I am not suggesting that we should abandon all our traditional Christian language, although metaphorical language is in even greater danger of becoming obsolete and meaningless than plain factual language, which incidentally has often its own hidden metaphors. What we must do is to make it quite clear that we realise the limitations of the language we use. Scientists escape many language difficulties by using a technical jargon which only scientists of their particular sphere understand. Preachers cannot do this; they must use the common speech of their listeners—'grace' and 'love', 'person' and 'nature', but there needs to be a constant sensitivity to the changing nuances of meaning in these words. This sensitivity has been encouraged by the great emphasis in recent years on the study of biblical words, and, although this seems to be going a little out of fashion today, preachers and students have still much to gain from it.

A non-biblical word that gives much trouble is the word 'supernatural'. It arouses in our minds suggestions of ghosts and wizards and the occult, things in which educated people find it increasingly difficult to believe. If the 'supernatural' indicates what cannot be explained by science then its sphere is steadily diminishing. What we should be thinking of is not a contrast between what can and cannot be explained but a contrast more analogous to that between the conscious and the unconscious mind. Modern psychologists do not deny the reality of either; what they say is that what we are conscious of is merely as it were the surface of a much larger psychical reality, known only indirectly but in some ways determining those aspects of mind of which we are conscious. So believers hold that behind the facts known to science and largely determining these facts is the being commonly known as God. Even some agnostics would accept this, but what Christians would add from their knowledge of the revelation in Christ is that this reality is personal and so concerned with our human affairs that one New Testament writer could say enigmatically, 'God is love.'

CHAPTER THREE

The God of Revelation

If we are right that the existence and nature of God cannot be inferred from what is known of the universe, or from the aspirations of the human mind, then we must ask the question, 'Where, if anywhere, is God to be found?' My own answer would be: in the Judaeo-Christian tradition, as it is contained in the Holy Scriptures, and supremely in its record of the life, teaching, death, resurrection and continuing presence of Jesus Christ. Our direct knowledge of this tradition is almost exclusively limited to what is contained in the Bible. If I am accused, as I sometimes have been, of taking a 'narrowly biblical' view of our Christian faith, I can only reply that all the faith by which I live appears to have come to me directly or indirectly from this holy book. At the same time I strongly suspect that those who use the phrase 'narrowly biblical' have never read the Bible intelligently, or are intellectually incapable of doing so. Indeed the breadth of thought in the Bible—its plain matter-of-fact dealings with such 'improper' subjects as polygamy, adultery and sexual promiscuity might surprise many people even in this permissive age. If some of its incidents were depicted on the television screen there would certainly be an outcry from Mrs Whitehouse and others. Or again the Bible's sense of the majestic vastness and mystery of the universe—witness the last chapters of Job—suggest an anticipation of the space age rather than any literal fundamentalism. Above all its facing of the fundamental mysteries of life—the problem of suffering, the origin of evil, and the conquering power of love—give it the widest of scopes. Of course much of it is in language that is uncongenial today, and by that I mean more than what can be remedied by modern translations. When we want to disparage such language we call it the language of mythology or apocalyptic, and set it aside as incomprehensible, but it is fundamentally the language of all great poetry, and some of us believe that we get a richer and more profound truth from the great poets than we do from the scientists and historians, although they too have a part to play, and that part is also found in the Bible.

There has been in recent years a growing conviction in my mind that any real revival to come in the Church is to have as its secret and slogan, 'Back to the Bible' or rather 'Forward with the Bible'. This is what my very limited knowledge of Church history suggests. The great seminal thinkers of the Church, the men who have presented the gospel in a new and relevant way to their respective generations, like Augustine and Luther and Barth, have been outstanding Bible students. The sixteenth-century Reformation can be regarded as a 'back to the Bible' movement, and so can the new life that outside observers have seen in the Roman Church since Vatican II. Nor is it an accident that the places where the Church is growing in numbers to a large extent today are places where what some critics would call a 'narrowly biblical' Christianity is being preached.

There are three differences, I believe, required in our approach to the Bible today from, say, the approach of the sixteenth-century reformers. First of all it must be a critical approach in the best sense of that word. It has long been a puzzle to me that those who claim to take the Bible most seriously are often antipathetic to the use of those scientific and critical approaches that would be used in the study of any other great book that was regarded as of real significance for human life. I canot imagine, for example, that any mathematical philosopher swallows uncritically Russell and Whitehead's *Principia Mathematica*; the more seriously they take it the more they use their critical powers. Intelligent people are simply repelled by a glib and fanciful reconciliation of statements in the Bible that transparently contradict one another, and we have no right to raise such specious barriers against the acceptance of gospel truth. Honest laymen cannot accept certain passages in the Bible, even some relating to other things than the much publicised seven days of creation or the big fish that swallowed Jonah, as infallible accounts of the events of history or the facts of science. Faith in the Bible does not commit us to a pre-Copernican astronomy or to the Hellenistic view of a demon-haunted atmosphere. There are critics who have talked and still talk nonsense; I have already referred to their unguarded treatment of hypotheses and have suggested that this is common enough in other spheres. These rogue critics are condemned not because they have dared to question revealed truth, but because they have not used their critical tools properly. Where they are wrong they are to be proved wrong not by *ex-cathedra* pronouncements of Popes or dogmatic theologians; they are to be proved wrong by a more profound and intelligent criticism. For one like myself who was brought up in what might be called an open-minded evangelical tradition (and who has tried to stick to it!), the work of modern critical writers has made the Bible a more, and not a less, authoritative guide in both Christian doctrine and practical living. George Morrison of Wellington had a characteristic sermon on this, based, perhaps a little unfairly, on the text, 'Take away her battlements; for they are not the Lord's' (Jer. 5: 10). The Bible does not need the battlements indicated by such phrases as 'verbal inspiration' or 'fundamentalism' to defend itself against a purely destructive criticism.

Another difference required in our approach today, and here our difference is from some later evangelicals rather than from the Reformers, is that we should see the Bible not merely as God's word to the individual, and particularly to that aspect of the individual we mistakenly label as his religious life, but as

God's word to all mankind in every relationship of life. I suggested in my first chapter that if we mean by religion only those rather unusual practices and loyalties, with which other institutions in the modern world do not deal, then it is very doubtful whether religion is worth continuing as a human activity. The Bible certainly never makes the mistake of limiting religion to what a man does with his solitude, which was, I believe, A. N. Whitehead's account of religion. The Bible deals with such things as the making of war, the relation of a nation to an occupying power, the acquisition of money and the exploitation of the underprivileged. Some of the oracles of the Old Testament prophets are indeed labelled as 'concerning the nations'. There is of course a place for the inner life, and the Bible in the Psalms and the New Testament has plenty to tell us about this. Yet, until we see the Bible as God's word to business men, politicians, trade unionists, and in short to the whole world outside the closed huddles of the Church (as well as to those within), we are to miss much of real significance for today.

A third thing that we need to be reminded of today is that we ought to study the whole Bible, and not only those parts which fit in with our own religious outlook or our own schemes of salvation. The conservative evangelical, for example, from whatever part of Scripture he picks his text, often seems to me to limit the matter of his preaching to a few chapters of Romans and Galatians with some selections from Hebrews. Similarly the preacher of the social gospel seems to take his message largely from the synoptic gospels and, from the Johannine epistles and James. It will be probably more clear to others who read this book than it is to myself from what limited portions of Scripture I have derived my own beliefs. Of course what the majority of preachers say is true; what seems wrong is that they tend to identify their own particular selective outlook with the whole of biblical revelation. How little one hears from our pulpits of the cosmic Christ, so clearly presented in Colossians and Ephesians, or of what we may call the apocalyptic Christ, the subject not only of Revelation, but also of parts of the gospels and of Paul's letters. This selectivity has one unfortunate consequence which is illustrated in the example I have just given. Those, who in reaction from the common neglect of the apocalyptic teachings of the Bible have put much weight on them, have so often become crack-pots, calculating in disobedience to our Lord the date of the end of the world, and finding prophecy fulfilled in the oddest events. Something similar has happened to the biblical teaching about the Holy Spirit. It has been so much neglected by the general run of preachers that it has at times become the province of rather eccentric Christians, who, in spite of Paul's warnings, tend to lay emphasis on the external signs of the Holy Spirit rather than the inner reality. One way of extending our grasp of the varied teachings of the Bible is a systematic observing of the Christian year. Learned theologians, as well as simple preachers, can fall into error here. When a distinguished scholar wrote, 'In a sense . . . there is no such thing as a Christian ethic',[1] he himself knew what he meant. Lesser men under the influence of such a statement are apt to decry all ethical teaching as moralism.

Of course I am not for a moment suggesting that all passages of Holy Scripture are of equal importance; indeed what I have said about the need of a critical approach implies the opposite. No one but a fool imagines that the list of tabernacle furnishings in Exodus is as important as the Sermon on the Mount, or that the genealogical lists in Chronicles (and, let us not forget it, in two of the gospels) are of equal significance to Paul's resurrection hymn in First Corinthians, chapter 15. Fortunately the Bible itself suggests, and Christian theology has maintained,

---

[1] D. M. Baillie: *God was in Christ* (Faber, 1948), p. 115.

a simple but definite criterion in this matter. Jesus himself hinted that the value of Old Testament scriptures for his followers is that they testify of him (John 5: 39), and in the Johannine writings the familiar phrase for Scripture, 'the Word of God' indicates Christ himself rather than any written word. It is as other parts of the Bible point to Christ and measure up to his teaching and example that we are to judge their relative importance. In dealing with the Old Testament we must distinguish between a contrived and a natural witness to Christ. There have been people who have claimed that they can find a witness to Christ in every single verse of the Old Testament. This seems to me a piece of nonsense based on a false view of biblical inspiration. I myself have not found even the traditional interpretation of the seed of the woman bruising the serpent's head (Gen. 3: 15) a convincing prediction of the work of Christ. What I have seen is that the prophetic anticipations of the anointed king and the suffering servant and the apocalyptic son of man have been more than fulfilled in Jesus of Nazareth, although perhaps not always in the way that the prophets expected. Besides much of the Old Testament speaks to me of the same love of God to sinful men and of the possibility of men joyfully responding to that love which was to be more adequately and fully shown in Jesus Christ. It is through him that I know the love of God, and all the rest of the Scriptures are a kind of luminous background to the coming of Christ, adding here and there other insights to that revelation, but never providing a substitute for it.

The question is inevitably asked whether God has revealed himself outside Holy Scripture, in the books of other great religions as well as in that of our Judaeo-Christian tradition. I see no reason to answer, 'No' categorically. All I can say that it is not through them that God has revealed himself to me, and when I have been tempted to raise in my own mind theoretical questions of salvation apart from Christ, I seem to hear Jesus saying what he said to Peter asking too curiously about the fate of the beloved disciple, 'What is that to you? Follow me.'

CHAPTER FOUR

Ecce Homo

Many of us who were brought up in Christian homes believe in the Christian revelation without ever having had the kind of mystical experience that we commonly associate with the word 'revelation'. We believe in God and Christ because our parents and other people who influenced us as children believed in the God of the Bible and the gospel story. This was, I am convinced, the beginning of Christian faith in my own case, and it is not an unworthy or unreasonable beginning. My parents, by the faithfulness they showed in the worship and service of God, and by their lives generally, seem to me to have been people far more worthy of being believed than many of the clever people who have told me since that there is no God. For it was not merely that my parents had in turn taken their belief in God from their own parents, although undoubtedly in part they had. In lives often threatened by poverty, sickness and sorrow, they had tested their beliefs, and had found that God did not fail them—that he was all and more than all that their parents had told them. And in my own unworthy way, a rather faltering one as this book makes too clear, I have found that what my parents told me fits in with my own experience of life.

All this may suggest that my Christianity, and that of many like me, is a very second-hand affair. Indeed it might have been so if it were not for Jesus Christ, about whom my parents told me stories, and teachers later taught me, and I soon read for myself. For there was something very fascinating about this Jesus even to a small child. It is probably impossible for an adult to recall at all accurately in what this fascination consisted, but I think it had probably more to do with odd instances like Jesus walking on the sea and healing a man who had been rather mysteriously lowered from a roof than with Jesus taking the little ones in his arms and blessing them—the kind of story which adults think suitable for introducing children to their saviour. The strange thing about this fascination is that, while other infantile hero-worships have disappeared with growing knowledge, this one has grown and developed. In a devout home I was soon infected with a certain awe of Jesus and God. I certainly felt a sense of awesome mystery when I was taken as a child to witness the sacrament of the Lord's Supper, and I venture to think that seeing the sacrament is the best approach for any child to the broken body and shed blood of Christ and so to the central mystery of the crucifixion. Be that as it may I hold that the custom which has grown in our Presbyterian churches of practically debarring children from being present at communion services is thoroughly evil. It may be that, as this sense of mystery developed, there was a tendency to have a rather stained-glass picture of Jesus. It was T. R. Glover and those who followed the teaching of his *Jesus of History* who, in my generation made young people see Jesus as a person real and vibrant and responsive to our twentieth-century needs—'a man living upon victuals', as Carlyle said of Richard Coeur-de-Lion. We know now that while Glover's account was true as far as it went, it left out much of what the four gospels tell us of Jesus. Glover himself was well aware that there was more in Jesus than he had described. 'He eludes us, goes far out beyond what we can grasp or conceive, and I think the education of the Christian man or woman begins anew, when we realise how little we know about Jesus.'[1]

What can we know about Jesus today? There appear to be two basically different approaches to the Gospel records. Some people like myself tend to accept what is in the record unless they see good reason for rejecting it. Those of us who make even very limited claims to New Testament scholarship will try

---

[1] T. R. Glover: *The Jesus of History* (London, 1917), p. 174.

to apply the same critical standards as we would to any other ancient documents, say, what Xenophon and Plato wrote of Socrates. Other people, and they comprise many of our best New Testament scholars, tend to accept only those things in the New Testament record for which they can provide substantial logical or historical justification. The criteria which some of these scholars use seem to me very unsatisfactory. They hold for example that a reported saying of Jesus can be guaranteed to be a genuine word of the historical Jesus only if a close parallel to it is found neither in contemporary Judaism nor in the extra-canonical documents of the early Christian Church. My own experience as a teacher would suggest an almost opposite criterion. If Jesus could make a point in language familiar to his hearers, as he is sometimes reported doing from Old Testament sources, then he would certainly do so. Again would it not be the natural desire of his later followers to echo his actual words in their teachings and writings as we still try to do in our sermons?

If we accept, as most students now do, that our present gospels were composed in part at least from earlier sources two things seem to follow. First, these earlier sources, whether written or oral, are more likely to have contained reasonably accurate reports of eyewitnesses than books composed some thirty years later. Again, if these sources represent, as scholars suggest, the traditions of different Christian groups, the fact that they agree substantially in their accounts of certain incidents, e.g. the feeding of the five thousand, would be regarded as at least in some measure confirming the historicity of the event described. Two further considerations support my rather conservative views. I remember how the late Principal Taylor of Aberdeen, himself an experienced advocate, pointed out how many of the small details or asides in the gospel narratives were just what a lawyer would regard as confirming the truthfulness and accuracy of a witness's evidence; he instanced the 'sitting down' of Matthew 27: 36 as an example. The other consideration is from my own experience; as one gets older, one remembers outstanding experiences of one's youth, by no means accurately in every detail, but seeing them in a far truer perspective than one did at the time they happened. I think this is by and large true of all the gospel writers, but particularly the author of the fourth gospel. He is almost certainly at places not giving the actual words of Jesus, but his portrait of Jesus seems to me to be in greater depth and so in a way more true than that of the other three evangelists.

One finding of modern scholarship appears to me most convincing. The gospel writers and to a great extent their earlier sources see the earthly life of Jesus through what has been called the prism of Easter, believing with all their hearts that the Jesus of whom they are writing is the risen and exalted Christ. An inference is sometimes made from this that we have in the gospels a 'glorified' account of the life of Jesus rather than one that is historically reliable. But is it not possible and even likely that with their hind-sight after Easter the disciples saw the events of the life and the teaching of Jesus more truly than at the time they first knew them?

Where I differ from many of my conservative evangelical friends is that I am ready to be convinced that the reasonable probabilities against certain narratives being historically accurate demand my assent. I think it, for example, extremely likely that the story of the coin found in the fish's mouth (Matt. 17: 24-27) is a misunderstanding of teaching given in figurative language, and that some of the details in Matthew's crucifixion and resurrection narratives are later interpretations rather than the evidence of eye-witnesses. I realise, however, that my suggestions on these matters are only hypotheses, and I rejoice that for me the reasonable probability is that we have a basically true if incomplete picture of the historical Jesus.

Throughout its history the Church has vacillated in its thinking between the belief that Jesus was divine 'very God of very God' and the belief that he was human—'O son of man, our hero strong and tender.' I have shared this hesitation as I think every Christian must, except when he is writing text-books of theology. When I spoke about this to Indian students, I used to say that God showed himself to man in Jesus of Nazareth as far as this was possible under the limitations of a human body and a human mind. By and large this is still my belief although I realise that it probably leads me into one or other of those heresies of the early church to which historians have given long names which I fail to remember accurately. Later reflection makes me add one or two comments. If God, as our Judaeo-Christian tradition maintains, created man in some sense 'in his own image', it does not seem as absurd as some people think it to be, that he should reveal himself in a man. Again this account may not do justice to certain aspects of the historical Jesus—the superhuman authority with which he spoke and acted, the dread that his presence sometimes aroused in those who confronted him, and his performing of those 'uncanny' events that we call 'miracles', but which the New Testament usually with more significance labels 'works of power' or 'signs'. Such things do seem beyond the capacities of an ordinary human body and an ordinary human mind. Yet I wonder, if other men were to show the same whole-hearted obedience to the will of the heavenly Father as Jesus did, whether they too would not perform miracles and show an unexpected authority. Jesus himself seems to have expected his followers to do such strange things, and some of them apparently did so in the first century and, somewhat occasionally, ever since. The Bible states explicitly that Jesus 'increased in wisdom', 'learned obedience', and as a boy asked questions (presumably honest religious questions) of the teachers in the temple. This implies that he shared the accepted views of his time not only about historical and scientific matters, but even about such partially religious questions as the historicity of the Old Testament and the like. What we can believe is that the sinless Jesus heard God speaking to him through the words of the Old Testament and in other ways with a clarity and directness that no other human being has experienced. If my account of Jesus as both God and man has any merit, it is in abandoning such words as 'nature', 'person' and 'substance' and their Greek and Latin near-equivalents, which were, no doubt, at one time understood by scholarly people, but which are largely meaningless today even to intelligent people. In our teaching and preaching we must certainly get rid of them.

What then can we know of God from what we know of the Jesus of history? Today we are often told that Jesus was supremely 'a man for others', and in this he is surely not merely an example for our human conduct, but a revelation of God's personal, loving concern for each one of his human children. Again Jesus suffered both by actual injury and by sorrow of heart because of the sins of men. Even the Hebrew prophets knew that 'in all their affliction God was afflicted' (Isa. 63: 9), and it is impossible after Good Friday to retain any Greek notions of the impassibility of God. Thirdly, and this is something that humanists often despise in the gospel, Jesus condemned evil in language which sometimes seems exaggerated and cruel to our Western ears, but which shows, in language that we can understand, God's attitude to evil. Many have thought of this revelation as a necessary prelude to the revelation given on the cross, but we shall leave this to our next chapter. Jesus was, again, the giver of life, noticing and often satisfying the common needs of ordinary people—hungry people, sick people, bereaved people and the like, and that this was a revelation of what God does is confirmed in the experience of many believers, although here we have the very baffling problem of why God permits human suffering to continue, and indeed allowed the human Jesus to share to an apparently extreme degree in these sufferings. But what has appealed to me most of all in recent years is Jesus' revelation of the faithfulness and trustworthiness of God. He was what he was because he knew God as his father completely reliable and worthy of obedience, even when human reason raises doubts and difficulties. It is because Jesus could say with his whole being, 'I know whom I have believed' that Paul and many others who have tried to follow Jesus can say the same.

CHAPTER FIVE

Christ Died for Our Sins

In traditional evangelical preaching it was commonly assumed that a conviction of one's own sinfulness was a necessary prelude to accepting Christ and committing oneself to him. Undoubtedly this has been the pattern of many conversions, but an admittedly limited intercourse with new converts in India suggests to me that people sometimes come to Christ in other ways. They may be led to him, for example, by the attractiveness of his personality, or even by the good fellowship seen among Christians, as a friend from a Hindu background once suggested to me. In many cases a conviction of sin came later and it seems likely that everyone who comes into living contact with Christ will sooner or later feel his own unworthiness to share Christ's fellowship.

There has been recently a reaction against what Banhoeffer called the evangelist's 'poking and prying into the insides of men' and many of us see a real danger here in the methods of certain evangelists. It would certainly be wrong to arouse in men a sense of individual guilt, when the individual rightly or wrongly holds that he has done no wrong, and then to offer them a deliverance for which they felt no need until they fell under the evangelist's spell. It may be a comfort to Christians to know that in Bonhoeffer's eyes the worst offenders here are not Christian preachers but existential philosophers and psycho-analysts with their 'secularised methodism'.[1]

There certainly can be a morbid sense of sin, and to some extent during a rather prolonged adolescence I shared in it. But there is nothing morbid about facing facts, and the fact is that there are flagrant evils in the world today recognisable

---

[1] D. Bonhoeffer: *Letters and Papers from Prison* (Fontana, 1959), p. 156.

even by the least introspective—the exploitation of the underprivileged, the crimes of violent cruelty that fill our prisons, the murder of people of other nations hypocritically described as 'a just war', and the hard pornography that deliberately corrupts young people for financial gain. I do not need to be a psycho-analyst to know that, with many other circumstantial factors, the basic cause of these and other evils is the selfishness and lack of concern for others that I see so often, if I would only look, in my own thoughts and actions. The facts of both history and my own personal experience demonstrate that such selfishness tends to bring suffering and disaster to the human race, not only at times to the selfish man himself, as moralists would like it to be, but even more obviously to others. It is very strange that this generation has so largely abandoned the biblical teaching of hell, however spiritually conceived, when the wickedness and selfishness of men have led to such conspicuous hells as Auschwitz and Hiroshima, which exceed in their horror the most lurid pictures of hell in medieval art and literature. Carlyle was making a true point about this universe, perhaps in exaggerated language, when he wrote, 'Judgment for an evil thing is many times delayed, some day or two, some century or two, but it is sure as life, it is sure as death.'[1] Yet, even in face of all this evil, I cannot share the Calvinist's belief in total human depravity. I have seen too much kindness and helpfulness and courage in people who make no claim to be Christian believers to deny that they too, having been made in the image of God, reflect each in his own measure the divine love.

In Christian teaching the cross of Christ has been regarded as the place where the evil in the hearts of individual men, and so ultimately the evil in the whole world have been met, forgiven and overcome by the action of God. While I realise that this

---

[1] *Past and Present* (London, 1843), p. 11.

teaching is central to the Christian faith I profess, and one that grips the innermost core of my being, I do not find it easily defended by cool reasoning. The wickedness of men has been generally as conspicuous since AD 30, if that were the year of the crucifixion, as it was before that date, and individuals who have with more or less understanding put their trust in Christ crucified do not appear in many cases, although certainly in some, to have won a dramatic victory over evil. I had in my youth a too limited picture of what should happen in the Christian life. When a man looked in faith upon the cross of Christ, as Bunyan's Christian did, a great burden should fall off his back and be seen no more, although it was not very clear whether the burden of which the converted man gets rid is a burden of guilt or, as I imagined, the oppressive weight of the sinful tendencies of human nature. Personally I have known no such dramatic experience. It is true that, as the years have passed, some bad habits and evil tendencies have to a greater or less extent left me, but I am sure that psychologists would attribute any such limited moral improvements to a natural growth in maturity and to the practical discipline of living, and so long as they admit that these factors are in the hands of God and used by him, I am inclined to agree with them. For many years I envied those who could look back to a dramatic experience of conversion. I am now reconciled to the fact that this has not been God's way for me. I realise that for one of my temperament such an experience might well have encouraged that concentration on self and on one's own welfare which I regard as the antithesis of that denial of self to which the man who like Paul has been crucified with Christ is called. I have known some whose conversion experience seems outwardly at any rate to have made them more self-assertive, while I have known others with no claim to such an experience who have lost all concern for self. It is this kind of self-denial that I long to find from the cross of Christ.

Of course sounder theologians maintain that what we receive at the moment of a trustful commitment to Christ is God's forgiveness realised in a sense of deliverance from the guilt of sin, and that victory over temptation, or sanctification as it used to be called, comes later and often very gradually. Yet I still cannot answer the question why the cross of Christ was a necessary condition of God bestowing or man receiving such forgiveness. The writer of the 103rd psalm—one that is very dear to me—apparently knew that God was forgiving all his iniquities without his knowing anything of the cross of Christ. And all the attempted explanations of what Christ did on the cross to secure the forgiveness of our sins seem to me to be in danger of blasphemously finding a kind of schizophrenia in the being of God, as if there were a contrast between God's justice and God's mercy. This I cannot accept, but I do believe that my sins are forgiven, and I believe, not from any convincing argument but from a kind of growing insight (which psychologists would say was due to my having been so conditioned in my youth) that this forgiveness is bound up with what happened on Good Friday. What this forgiveness means practically is that we need to have no regrets over our misspent past, and that each day we can make by the grace of God a new start in life, 'be born again every morning', as an evangelist once described to me his experience of life. I find it very sad when I hear old people still grieving over the sins of their youth, which have been forgiven and should have been forgotten long ago. The blame for this often lies with clergymen, who in their leading of congregational worship sometimes appear to forget that complete and final absolution for his own and his congregation's sins was sought and pronounced on the previous Sunday, if not even more recently.

It is not only forgiveness that men have found in the cross of Christ, but Christian morality finds example, inspiration and power in an ever firmer holding on to Christ crucified. The moral victory that is distinctively Christian is the denial of self. 'If any man would come after me,' said Jesus, 'let him deny himself and take up his cross, and follow me.' To put others before one's self and to put God's will, however it is known, before one's own will is not only following the example of Jesus; it is a kind of integration with Christ crucified, a living experience that in the cross of Christ the world is crucified to me, and I to the world. How far some of us are from this condition I know too well, and yet I think I am right in not being satisfied with the assurance that 'the great transaction's done' at some moment of conversion. Certainly God did his part in my salvation on the first Good Friday, but I still feel that I shall only be truly saved (to use the familiar evangelical term) when I can honestly say with Paul, 'Not I but Christ in me.'

Many of my own and other people's intellectual difficulties here may be due to a too literal acceptance of the metaphors with which Paul and others have tried to describe what Christ did for sinful men on the cross—receiving a judicial punishment which ought to have been ours, paying the ransom price necessary to secure our freedom from the tyranny of sin, offering himself as a propitiatory sacrifice like the sacrificial animals in the old Israelite cultus, and fighting and winning in a very real way a battle against the spiritual powers of evil in this universe. The last is probably the metaphor which appeals to me most. What I believe is rightly indicated in all these metaphors is that Jesus did for us on the cross something real and objective in God's dealing with men, and that this was not merely, as the fashionable moral theory of today suggests, a method of arousing in us the pious feelings and resolutions that we ought to feel to a God of immeasurable love. The various metaphors may well indicate the nearest human analogies to different aspects of what was a unique, once-for-all event. The danger of every one of them, and it is a danger of which contemporary studies of language have made some of us very conscious, is the tendency to speak of something that is literally ineffable as if it were almost a mechanical business transaction like the payment of a debt demanded by a usurer or, worse still, the bribery of a judge by a gift pleasing to him. Whatever explanation we may try to offer of what Christ did on the cross, it must be in terms of personal love—the love of Christ for his disciples, the love of the Father for men, however sinful, and the love that the Holy Spirit pours into human hearts. I, alas, have not found an explanation which satisfies me, but this does not prevent me from being moved in the depths of my being as I look on the crucified Christ, particularly as he is shown and indeed given to me in the broken bread and poured-out wine of the Lord's Supper.

While I have had in this chapter to confess my own lack of understanding, this does not hinder me from placing such faith as I have on Christ crucified, and acknowledging that other men's intellectual insights which I have some difficulty in sharing may be true. I take to myself for my own encouragement the words of Dr R. W. Dale who wrote a great book on the atonement, 'I have been thinking about it and preaching about it for more than forty years, and yet there seem to be vast provinces of truth in it which I am only just beginning to explore.'

CHAPTER SIX

The Lord is Risen

No competent historian would deny that Jesus of Nazareth was put to death by crucifixion probably on a Friday in the spring of a year round about AD 30, although when they hear Paul's testimony that Christ 'died *for our sins*', they would in all probability rightly say that as historians we know nothing about that and must leave the matter to the theologians. When it comes to what traditionally happened on the following Sunday, that 'he was raised on the third day', historians are naturally more sceptical, although Paul clearly held that his belief in the resurrection depended on the historical evidence given by eye-witnesses (I Cor.: 15. 3–8). There is a tendency today to consider that it is possible to believe in the spiritual truth represented by the resurrection stories without believing that anything historically verifiable happened on Easter day. That is a view I cannot share; just as the doctrine of the atonement would be meaningless for me without a historical crucifixion so the Christian hope of life beyond death would be largely meaningless to me, as it apparently was to Paul, without the historical resurrection of Jesus. My own conviction is that, even if we were to discount some of the gospel narratives as later additions to the story, there is still strong ground for our believing as historians that the Jesus who was crucified was seen to be alive on Easter day and after. Among the various items of evidence, the two that convince me most are (*a*) the list of eye-witnesses (some still alive, so that they could be examined) given by Paul within twenty-five years of the event, and (*b*) the transformation that took place in the band of followers after the death of Jesus. C. D. Broad, who was certainly not a biased critic, said that 'something very queer happened soon after the crucifixion which led certain of his disciples and Paul to believe that Jesus had survived in some supernatural way.'[1] My own judgment is that the very queer thing that happened was the resurrection.

There are thinkers, both conservative and radical, who appear to assume that if the resurrection was an historical event it was necessarily what they call a physical event. I heard recently a preacher say in an Easter sermon that those who did not believe in a physical resurrection were not Christians. Yet a body which had according to the gospel narratives the power to disappear and to reappear in a room with closed doors is not what we usually understand by a physical body. The fact that Paul considers his own experience on the Damascus road, which many would describe as a vision, as equal to the Easter experiences of the earlier apostles, suggests something more than a physical event. What is even more significant is that neither at Easter nor on the Damascus road is Christ indicated as showing himself to others (with the exception of Paul) than those who had faith in him.

The gospel accounts certainly maintain that the body of the risen Christ had certain of the characteristics of a physical body. Jesus spoke to and ate with his disciples, and the invitation to touch as well as see that body indicates something physical. Many scholars today think of the story of the empty tomb as a later elaboration, but the early gospel account in Mark with its statement, 'He is not here', and the implication in Paul's argument that what was buried (certainly a body) was raised again convince me that the empty tomb was an historical fact. That a number of his followers recognised the risen Lord (although in some cases not as immediately as one might expect) suggests that they at least believed they were in contact with the same physical body. I should like to say that what rose

---

[1] C. D. Broad: *Religion, Philosophy and Psychical Research* (London, 1953), p. 230.

from the grave was what Paul calls 'a spiritual body', but I realise that students of language would find such a term self-contradictory. When we are dealing with an event that we hold to be unique, we must not put it in the class of physical events like the resuscitation of a corpse, which would have little religious relevance or in the class of spiritual events, like visions or even hallucinations. It had some characteristics of both but was essentially something entirely new and unique.

What was important to the first disciples, and to us, is that the Jesus of Nazareth whom they had known, and whose death they had witnessed was alive and still with them in a very real if inexplicable way. At first their reaction was naturally enough one of terror. In the earliest account with any detail of what happened (in Mark 16: 1-8), there are no fewer than four different words to describe the women's fear. R. H. Lightfoot was probably right in maintaining that to those to whom the resurrection was thus revealed, 'at first the solid earth must have seemed to reel beneath their feet, and the stars to be about to fall.'[1] But this mood of terror seems to have quickly changed into a mood of joy, which lasted even when the disciples realised that Jesus was no longer to show himself, except in occasional vision to a few individual mystics, in a visible way. The resurrection stories have much of their significance as demonstrations that Jesus was with his disciples to the end of the age in their ordinary life and work—in the eating of ordinary meals, but especially in the breaking of bread at the Lord's Supper, in the practice of their ordinary business as fishermen, and most of all in their obedience to his challenge to witness and service, which is made explicit in a number of the narratives.

Two beliefs which stem from a belief in the resurrection, and which have meant much to me are the assurance of the real presence of Christ in the world, and the assurance of a life

---

[1] R. H. Lightfoot: *The Gospel Message of St Mark* (O.U.P., 1950), p. 96.

beyond death. About the first of these it is much easier to say what the real presence is not than what it is. It is, of course, not normally a visible presence as it was during Jesus' life on earth, or even in the spasmodic appearances for forty days or so after the Resurrection. Nor is it simply the undoubtedly true fact that Jesus' life and influence are at work in the world to a greater degree but still in the same fashion as the lives and influences of Socrates and Confucius are still at work in the world. I once wrote that we should think of Jesus as alive and active in the affairs of men in the way that Richard Nixon and Harold Wilson are alive and active, but that is obviously in one way incorrect. We can see Wilson and Nixon, but we cannot see Jesus. Nor do I mean the sense of 'a presence' which some Christians seem to enjoy much more than others who are equally or even more committed to Christ. It is no accident that the most vehement debate over Christ's living presence has been about his real presence in the sacrament, for whatever crude and unscriptural views have been held about this, they bear witness to the fact that it is in the sacrament that Christians down the ages have known that Christ was really with them. There are, we must admit, some Christians to whom the sacraments mean little, but Christ reveals himself to different men in different ways, for example, in the hearing of the Word and in prayer. Yet the really important thing is the knowledge that Christ is with us all the time, whether we are conscious of his presence or not. One of the things I have learned from Bonhoeffer is how Christ meets and challenges men even in the most worldly situations. He still bids us to come and dine, and to cast our nets. When I write in my next chapter about the Holy Spirit, I shall suggest that one function of the Spirit is to enable us to see the Jesus of the gospels still guiding our lives.

There has been much confusion between the Christian doctrine of resurrection and the Greek doctrine of the immortality of the soul. At one time I would have argued with conviction that there is no biblical or indeed philosophical ground for believing in a natural and universal human immortality. The only promise of life after death is made to believers and apocalyptic references to 'the second death' point to the extinction of those who have no part in eternal life. It may be best, I would have argued, to put a derelict human soul out of pain, just as we charitably put a suffering animal out of pain, and this would seem to be a more acceptable picture of the fate of the damned than the conventional one derived from Jerusalem's burning rubbish-heaps. Yet I am now more uncertain about this, for as I attend the funerals of some of my friends who have apparently been unable to accept the Christian gospel, I cannot but feel that such 'sweet and virtuous souls' had something of the quality of Herbert's 'seasoned timber', and cannot have been blotted out in a universe that has real meaning (as Christians hold), however little we may comprehend that meaning now. At any rate we can only commend such people to the love and mercy of God of which we, as believers, have so much need ourselves.

During my adolescence when the words 'the resurrection of the body' were recited in the creed, with some honesty and perhaps more arrogance, I closed my lips in silence. I could not believe that putrefying corpses soon to disintegrate into dust would be miraculously revivified. I had obviously not read with any understanding the fifteenth chapter of First Corinthians in which Paul makes it clear that the body which is raised is a very different body from that which is buried, although there is some mysterious element of continuity with it. Now when many of those dearest to me have departed this life (a most pleasing, if archaic, way of putting it), I find the doctrine of the resurrection of the body most comforting and reassuring. It speaks not of the poor done body which will soon be earth, but of the whole personality, and not an abstracted soul, being expressed in a new body of a new kind. Indeed this is what we might expect, for what is most precious in each human being is his unique personality, and those who argue that death means an absorption in the infinite or the like are leaving out one of the things that I desire most in a life after death—the joy of human intercourse. Of course this is wishful thinking, but, since the resurrection of Jesus it is wishful thinking based on historical fact and reasoned argument, as Paul so cogently demonstrated in First Corinthians, chapter 15. I realise that Paul's argument needs to be rewritten in modern terms and in the light of modern studies of human personality if it is to be generally convincing. Even in its present old-fashioned setting I cannot doubt its validity.

I have left out so far what many theologians would regard as the most important thing about the resurrection, namely that by it God vindicated Christ and what he had done on the cross. There are times that I have been attracted to the heretical teaching, suggested but not affirmed in Romans 1: 4, that it was in his being raised from the dead that the man Jesus attained divinity. What is true in this suggestion is that, in spite of his sinlessness, in spite of the authority of his teachings and actions, in spite of his miracles, and in spite of his clearly expressed claims of divine sonship (found not only in the fourth gospel but in the older saying, recorded in Matthew 11: 27 and Luke 10: 22), apart from the resurrection Jesus might still be regarded as merely a good and great man—a man stretched to the very limit of human excellence. Of course he was that, but after the resurrection his first followers knew, and I know, that he is the risen and glorified Lord, no longer to be known 'after the flesh', but as 'my Lord and my God'. As I have already suggested, his whole life, which was in all respects a real human life, can now be seen in a richer and truer way as the life of God living as man among men. Best of all his death on the cross can be seen not as a pathetic martyrdom, but as an event of cosmic significance winning in some way that I do not understand a new kind of life for men both here and in the here-after. The true symbol of our salvation is not the crucifix with our Lord broken and bleeding as we often see it in Roman churches; it is rather the figure of the risen Lord, exultant and triumphant, standing out from the cross as the source of his glory. It is to Christ crucified *and risen* that we owe our salvation.

The resurrection, and more frequently, the ascension of Jesus have been regarded as evidence that the humanity of Jesus is now in the presence and indeed in the very being of God. This is something which theologians have used a difficult theological jargon to express. The Creed says that 'he sitteth at the right hand of God the Father Almighty,' and the writer of Hebrews pictures 'our great high priest having passed into the heavens'; both are clearly using highly figurative language. It is the Scottish paraphrase of the Hebrews passage which expresses best what this teaching has meant to me,

> Though now ascended up on high,
> He bends on earth a brother's eye;
>
> . . . . . .
>
> Our fellow-sufferer yet retains
> A fellow-feeling of our pains.

To put it in more modern words, there is an understanding of our human predicament based on genuinely human experience in the mind and being of God. That is a belief, I consider, unique to the Christian faith, and very comforting to my own soul.

CHAPTER SEVEN

The Holy Spirit

Many Christians would, I think, feel uncomfortable if Paul's question to the Ephesian disciples were put to them, 'Did you receive the Holy Spirit when you believed?' I myself would answer 'Yes' rather hesitatingly. Yes, I must have received the Holy Spirit; otherwise I could not have put my trust in Christ as I have done however falteringly. Yet I have had no pentecostal experience, as the first disciples certainly had, and I have none of those gifts of miracle-working or speaking with tongues which provided evidence in the first century that some people had received the Holy Spirit. I have come to believe that the best test for possession of the Spirit was indicated by Jesus in his teaching in the upper room, 'The spirit of truth will bear witness to me'; 'He will glorify me, for he will take what is mine and declare it to you'. The man whose thoughts, feelings and will are directed towards Jesus can be quite sure that the Holy Spirit is at work in his life.

Two other factors have contributed to the reluctance with which many Christians speak of the Holy Spirit. The one is the old name, 'the Holy Ghost', for to modern ears the good old English word 'ghost' suggests something superstitious and unreal—supernatural in the bad sense! We should get rid of it from our Christian vocabulary. The other factor is that, from the day of Pentecost onwards, the Holy Spirit has been associated with behaviour that has appeared unseemly to the conventional—men drunk at nine o'clock in the morning, and the like.

There are, I believe, more familiar experiences in life in which we are conscious of the guidance of the Holy Spirit. When one is faced with an important decision, one uses of course one's common sense or one seems to be compelled by circumstances, but in these things too the Holy Spirit has a part. One of the happy things in my own life has been the assurance (in Archbishop Trench's words),

> Thou cam'st not to this place by accident,
> It is the very place God meant for thee.

Of course this does not mean that one stays in the same place throughout life; one may have the same kind of guidance to move elsewhere or change one's occupation, (as I have twice done). The modern world seems often to demand such changes, and the old idea of a vocation for life has lost its power in a rapidly changing world. One thing I can testify from experience (and there has been too little of such personal witness in this book) is that, when I have honestly sought God's guidance in prayer, that guidance has been given me, not in mystical fashion by a voice from heaven, but by the right course of action becoming clear to my own mind. I could give no better advice to people of a younger generation who have decisions to make about work or marriage or the like, than that they should honestly and simply ask for guidance from God in prayer. It is my experience that the Holy Spirit will usually provide it.

Another activity of the Holy Spirit is to give men strength and courage to face the troubles of life—sickness, sorrow, disappointment and disillusionment. Most ministers have had the experience of going to visit bereaved people, whom they had thought of as rather half-hearted Christians, and of finding that these people had already received a courage and serenity that were quite unexpected by themselves or by others. The Authorised Version translation of Christ's name for the Holy Spirit—the 'comforter', which had gone rather out of fashion among New Testament students in the first half of this century, is now recognised as having at least some justification. 'Comforter' seems to me very much better than the New English Bible 'counsellor', for what the Holy Spirit gives is not merely good advice, and not only sympathetic consolation, but a strength that is indicated by the Latin root *fortis* in the word 'comforter'. Of course once again the sceptics may offer a natural explanation of this unexpected access of strength. Even if they are right, I still believe that it is a gift of God's spirit in whatever way it comes.

It is natural for one who has spent much of his life in study to have a special liking for the other name that Jesus gave to the Holy Spirit—'the Spirit of Truth'. This name surely indicates that our searchings for the truth so often frustrated, and so often with apparently no practical outcome, are in accordance with God's will for us. Here again the witness to Christ in our minds leads us to him, who is the supreme truth—'the way, the truth and the life'.

In the Reformed tradition we have long held that it is the inner witness of the Holy Spirit which makes us hear in the words of Scripture God speaking to us. Without the work of the Spirit the words of the Bible would be ordinary human words as they are to so many unbelievers, and even at times to some of us who believe. Something similar is true of the sacraments. The Holy Spirit makes the water of Baptism and the bread and wine of the Supper not merely symbols to remind us of what Christ has done, but effective means of grace.

So far I have been considering some of the more general activities of the Holy Spirit, for which there is ample evidence in Holy Scripture and Christian experience. The Holy Spirit does come to men with a gentle voice

> 'That checks each fault, that calms each fear
> And speaks of heaven'

Yet no honest student of the Bible could believe that this is the whole truth about the Holy Spirit. In the Bible the Spirit comes more characteristically and excitingly in a mighty rushing wind and tongues of flame. The Whitsunday custom in some Italian churches of representing these tongues of flame by rose petals falling gently from the ceiling is perhaps symbolic of the way in which we have all tried to domesticate the Holy Spirit. The outcome of Pentecost was not merely the apostles' speaking in foreign languages but a mass conversion of some three thousand people. We who still preach about the Holy Spirit have seen nothing like that.

Many Christian people today must share my deep longing that there should be in our day such a dramatic outpouring of the Holy Spirit. It has happened in the past, as in the great American revival of 1859–1861, or in the Welsh revival of 1904, and it is happening in certain parts of the Church, particularly in South America, today. It may be that what looks to outsiders the rather sub-human activity of making unintelligible noises is necessary to keep men from trusting in their own knowledge and achievements. If we really want a pentecostal experience, we must be prepared to behave in ways that are generally regarded as not seemly for respectable Christians. Sociologists may be right in suggesting that speaking with tongues is a phenomenon most likely to occur among people less educated and more socially cohesive than people of the Western world today. Frankly I should not expect a much needed revival in a university senior common-room to be accompanied by what the dons would certainly call *glossolalia*. Yet when I watch on television the ways in which football crowds and spectators at a boxing contest display their enthusiasm over their idols, and see in a film pentecostalist Christians in Chile showing a rather similar behaviour in their worship, I wonder whether there would not be similar ongoings in Scotland if there was a real and widespread turning to God. Yet I cannot believe that speaking with tongues or any other abnormal phenomenon is a necessary indication of the presence of the Spirit as some pentecostalists suggest. The presence of the Holy Spirit in a genuine twentieth-century revival may be accompanied by very different signs from those of the first Pentecost, but they will probably be equally misunderstood and despised by the majority of men.

Paul appears to make a distinction between what he calls the fruit of the Spirit—love, joy, peace, patience, kindness, goodness, faithfulness, gentleness and self-control—qualities which should be found in every Christian, and gifts of the spirit or *charismata*, including such unusual things as speaking with tongues and miracle-working, which are certainly not given to every Christian. The Spirit 'apportions them to each individually as he wills'. Paul even thinks of outstanding faith as a *charisma* given to certain individuals (I Cor. 12: 9). One of the lessons which I have found hard to learn in life is that even with the best of intentions and an honest desire to use one's gifts in the service of God, there are some things one cannot do for lack of the necessary charisma. Preachers have sometimes assured me that 'I can do all things through Christ who strengthens me,' but if this means that I can sing in the Church choir or preach at a street-corner (which I have once or twice tried to do most ineffectively), they are taking the text out of its context. The 'all things' of which Paul is writing are ways of facing life's changing circumstances, and many Christians can bear witness to the sufficiency of God's grace for doing so. It is my belief, however, that God has given every Christian some special gift, and what may sound the humblest of Paul's *charismata*—the doing of acts of mercy with cheerfulness—is the one most akin to 'the more excellent way' of Christian love.

Ronald Knox ended his splendid book *Enthusiasm* with a quotation from *La Princesse lointaine* which haunted him as he wrote the book, and which has haunted me ever since I read it there:

FRÈRE TROPHIME: L'inertie est le seul vice, Maître Erasme,
   Et la seule vertu est . . .

ERASME: Quoi?
FRÈRE TROPHIME: L'enthousiasme!

And enthusiasm is the essential quality of the Holy Spirit and of spirit-filled men.

CHAPTER EIGHT

The Church of Christ

Can I honestly say, 'I believe in the Holy Catholic Church,' when I shall, in the present chapter, say so much that is critical of the methods and the members of the Church today? At least I am conscious that much of this criticism must be made of myself as a member of the Church, and particularly of my own work for five or six years as a parish minister. The tendency to criticise has been useful to me as a teacher and examiner, but it is a great hindrance to whole-hearted devotion and I find myself in the worship of the Church often criticising rather than learning and praying.

Yet I have little patience with those who say that they are Christian believers, and maintain they can be so without any real relationship to the Church. I once heard an Anglican padre making the point in an address to troops that a soldier, however loyal to queen and country, would be of very little use if he did not learn discipline and co-operation in the limits of his own platoon, company and regiment, and that this is true also of the service of Christ. There may be exceptional 'lone wolves', but most of us need the fellowship that the Church can give in its worship and service.

The Church has various functions, but not all are of the same importance. It serves the world in many ways and it may be God's challenge to it today, as Bonhoeffer suggests, to forget about the maintenance and welfare of its own traditional institutions and so to 'deny' itself in order to serve others. Even in a welfare state like our own there is still room for the Church and its people to do a great variety of things for the sake of others, things which my own Church of Scotland in its social service and the Salvation Army are very effectively doing.

In a country parish it was good to see that church members took the lead in many of the secular activities of the community, and in new housing areas it is the Church that leads in bringing about the fellowship that is so necessary for a new community. The Church has a work of education both for its own members and outsiders, and, as I have already suggested, it looks as if the Christian education of children is soon to be the work of the Church rather than of the school which has played so large a part in it in the past. The Church too provides a worthy setting for the great occasions of life—birth (in the sacrament of Baptism), marriage and death—a setting which many non-believers find attractive, and many rather hypocritically use in accordance with custom. The Church too makes efforts that others both in its own community and throughout the whole world should be presented with the challenge of the gospel. The rather patriarchal and patronising methods of Victorian missions both at home and abroad may be out of date, and rightly so, but the duty to preach the gospel to all nations is still there. Mission has been called the 'life-blood' of the Church, and many would regard evangelism—the making known of the gospel to all men in all the circumstances of life—as the Church's primary task.

I do not agree. The more we have of all these activities the better, but so many of them seem today to become man-directed activities in which humanists can often share. The Church is primarily a God-directed institution, and its first and most characteristic function is worship. Other institutions may share in social service and education, and in most respects the State is doing these things better than the Church did them in the past, but it is only the Church that worships. Worship is happily described in a recent report to the General Assembly of the Church of Scotland as 'our joyful response to God for all that he is in his own glory and has done for us in Jesus Christ.' This is something very different from the preaching of the Word, which has been the central and most prominent part of public worship in our Presbyterian tradition. There is of course a place in worship for reminding the worshippers of what God has done in order to stimulate the activity of worship, but this is secondary to worship itself. There were times in Scotland when the minister came into the Church to preach, after a reader had conducted what were rather blasphemously called the preliminaries, although surely praise and prayer are more worshipping activities than hearing sermons. I am still often invited to 'preach' in a Church when what I am really required to do is to lead the people in all their worship.

If New Testament scholars are right, there were two kinds of preaching in the early Church—to use the modern jargon, *kerygma*, 'the kind of speech which is likely to draw men into the Christian community', and *didache*, 'the kind of speech which is required for the further instruction of those who are within it'. Now there are preachers whose special *charisma* is the proclamation of the *kerygma*, and today the Church has increasingly to do this in a largely Pagan society. There are new means of doing so; radio and television have up till now provided in this country marvellous opportunities for proclaiming the good news to many, otherwise unlikely to hear it. There is still room for the Church to occupy along with other propagandists the traditional stands for open-air preaching; no one can belittle what Donald Soper has done at Tower Hill. What I am suggesting is that the Sunday morning service of worship is not normally the place for such *kerygma*. It may have been so in the past when many people were compelled to attend Church by public opinion and other pressures. Today the people inside the Church are for the most part those who have already honestly committed themselves to Christ admittedly with much still to learn of Christian truth. There are occasions, like the great days of the Christian year, when we need to be reminded of the basic tenets of our faith, and every celebration of the sacrament, and indeed every reading of the Word can be such a reminder. Yet I am convinced that what the usual congregation needs as its regular sustenance is not *kerygma* but *didache*, teaching for spiritual growth rather than challenge to repentance.

Modern educationists would question the common assumption that the sermon is the only or the best way of giving such teaching either to children or to adults. In university teaching, both internal and extramural, the regular lecture is being more and more displaced by the seminar or discussion group or 'teach-in', and I wonder whether the Church should not be looking for ways of teaching that are better than the sermon. I wonder too whether the weekly service of worship is the best setting for such teaching. It is good, for those who are being taught, to respond with a critical attitude of mind, but critical thoughts can be very destructive of devout worship, as I know to my cost.

The great problem of devising an order for public worship is that individual worshippers with their different temperaments naturally find some ways of making a joyful response to God more congenial than others. While I suggest that the basic Christian way of approach is the sacrament that has been long known as the Eucharist or thanksgiving, I realise that there are some true followers of Christ, who do not find the sacrament a means of grace for them, and are more helped by other forms of worship such as the singing of hymns—witness the popularity of the television programme of 'Songs of Praise'. I can only bear witness that some of my richest experiences in life have been at the table of the Lord, even although these have sometimes been spoiled by my own dryness of soul.

I have often played with ideas of what would be to me the best way of using a Sunday morning. I am naturally thinking of the kind of West End city church that I usually attend, and realise that other places would need a very different pattern.

I suspect too that many of my own fellow-members would not like the programme I am now suggesting. Here it is for better or worse:

9.30–10. The minister is available in the vestry for confessions, requests for prayer, and for giving spiritual counsel, but *not* for other matters.

10–10.45. This is the weekly service of worship, normally but not always the celebration of the Lord's Supper with the proclamation of the Word usually limited to the words of Scripture; there might be kerygmatic sermons on the great days of the Christian year. A clear proclamation of absolution should be made at an early point in the service so that the worshippers may, free from the burden of past sin, give themselves wholeheartedly to a joyful response both in the rest of their worship and in their ordinary lives afterwards. There should be much opportunity for the congregation to take a vocal part in prayer and praise, and mutual service (such as handing to each other the bread and wine of the sacrament). All should know that they are contributing something to the common worship.

10.45–11.15. This is a time for fellowship over a cup of coffee or the like. The minister is now available for more mundane concerns and this is his opportunity, or that of his session-clerk or some other officer to ask individuals to do certain things in the new week, such as visiting old Mrs Smith, or addressing envelopes for a War on Want appeal etc. I feel sure that such personal requests for particular services would get a better response than pulpit appeals for volunteers. Parents may use this half-hour to fetch for the time of teaching children who are not already at Church.

11.15–12. This is the time of teaching for all, from infants to senior citizens in as small groups as possible—something in the fashion of the old Methodist classes. The minister would normally at this time himself conduct the class of those preparing for Confirmation, but he would have already, perhaps on the previous Sunday evening, had preparation classes for those who lead the various groups, probably at least two classes, one for Sunday-school teachers, and another for those who are to lead adult groups. This kind of teaching should give a continuity of instruction that is often lacking between one sermon and the next. While many may not wish to attend a time of teaching every Sunday, they should be encouraged to do so regularly for a course of, say, ten weeks. These classes are not, except for very young children, services of worship, but each class might finish the morning with a brief epilogue.

A programme like this may seem out of place in a confession of faith, but it does indicate a strong conviction that the Church must rethink its methods of teaching and its forms of worship. Such a scheme will certainly not of itself bring people back to the Church; indeed one might think of it as a programme for the faithful remnant.

While I regard worship and particularly communal worship as the primary response to what God has done for us in Christ, I certainly believe that the necessary sequel should be what today is called 'mission', not quite the same thing as the missions of the past century. At one time the only activity that seemed to me worthy to be called mission was the direct proclamation of the gospel, but I should now regard almost any action done for the love of God, and love of the neighbour as a first step in mission, a first step, which should certainly lead to another when the believer should bear witness in words to the faith that is in him. What should be our concern is the best way of doing this in the late twentieth century. The constant repetition of the same challenge to the same audience in mission hall or gathered congregation seems to me of questionable value; there should come a time perhaps when the preacher should shake the dust off his feet and move to another city.

What a former Lord High Commissioner at the General Assembly once commended as 'speaking a good word for Jesus' in ordinary conversation with friends is probably the most effective kind of evangelism today. It is hard to know why many believers, including myself, are so diffident in speaking about Jesus. There is a natural, and not unseemly, reticence in talking about life's deepest experiences—the joys of marriage and the shame of failure as well as the contemplation of the Cross. Some of us make the excuse that we lack the evangelist's distinctive *charisma* but what we really need are not the orator's gifts but a freedom of speech in ordinary talk. Of course if all the Lord's people were to become prophets, as Moses once desired, our congregations might become miniature Bedlams, but this should not keep us from realising that there is some kind of witness in which every Christian should engage, the less self-consciously the better. It is the sin of despicable cowardice that commonly hinders us from doing so. I myself must bear an honest testimony that those who by their witness have helped me most on my spiritual journey were not generally people who proclaimed the gospel with most confidence and clarity, but those who, while struggling with doubts like my own, still held on to a strong faith in God as he is revealed in Christ.

What of the future of the Church? The decline in numbers of both members and regular worshippers was almost bound to happen in a century when public opinion no longer demands that every respectable person should be a church-goer, and when scientific humanism provides a reasonable, although to my mind a very dull, alternative to the Christian faith. One outcome of this is that the day for building large auditoria in the style of the traditional church is now past. What disturbs me more than our smaller numbers is the emphasis put on money in the courts of the Church, and the greater readiness of people in an affluent society to give money rather than worship and service. This is bound to corrode the spirituality of the church just as the love of money corrodes the spirituality of the individual. The fact is that I should see very little future for the organised church, if it were not for two things. The one is the power to survive which the Church has shown in the past in spite of worldly, and sometimes thoroughly wicked, ecclesiastics within and violent persecutors outside. The other is that I believe in the Holy Spirit, and this means that there will come a day, I know not when, which will see a new Pentecost.

CHAPTER NINE

Christian Living and Christian Loving

The present-day emphasis on love as the one guiding principle in Christian conduct is at the same time welcome as a return to basic New Testament teaching, and dangerous as liable to being misinterpreted in a variety of ways. All would agree that the love which is commended in the New Testament is different from much that is labelled love in the ancient as well as the modern world; this was probably the reason why the New Testament writers do not use the ordinary Greek words for love. The Bible makes it clear that love to God takes precedence over love to our fellow-men, and, if this is ignored, human love is apt to degenerate into sentimentality or sensuality. This love to God implies a whole-hearted response to what God has done for us in Christ. Jesus said, 'If you love me, you will keep my commandments.' He had probably in mind both the moral counsels he himself gave and the traditional ten commandments, and it is a marvel to me how relevant these ancient Jewish prohibitions and exhortations are to life in the modern world. If we love God, we try to do what God likes, not what we like—a needed correction to the often quoted and often misinterpreted maxim of St Augustine, 'Love and do what you like.' It is probably true that if we loved in the way that God loves and knew our fellow-men and their needs in the way that God knows them, then love would be the only necessary rule. However even the most high-principled and devout Christians are not like that; most of us do not love with the single-mindedness that we ought to have, and in our ignorance we so often say and do the wrong things to those whom we genuinely love. We certainly seem to need more guidance in the Christian life than that which is provided by love.

One of the pulpit cliches with which I disagree is, 'You must love, but need not like.' Love, we are told, is something commanded by Scripture, but our liking is an emotion which we cannot control. We cannot like people because we are told to do so. While I realise that we may, contrary to our Christian determination, feel a strong dislike of some of our fellow-men, I do not think that we should be content with this attitude. By praying for them, by showing a practical concern for their welfare, and by trying to get to know them better, we may encourage the incipient good-will which we practise as a Christian duty to grow into the fulness of Christian love which is properly characterised by warm affection. While I admit that I have dislikes which I have not altogether got rid of, I have had repeatedly, like many teachers, this happy experience. When I have met a class for the first time I have thought what a dull, uninteresting group they looked, but by the end of the session I have felt an individual interest and liking towards each attractive personality. A Roman scholar has recently put it in this way, 'Unless an attempt is made to resolve the emotional dislike, the love will not survive for long. . . . Christian love should normally involve liking, or at least gradually remove any disliking of persons.'[1]

In my reaction to modern permissiveness have I forgotten about Christian freedom, that we are called unto liberty and that Paul had freedom from a systematic code of moral as well as legal rules in mind when he wrote this? Yet the Bible as a whole, the teachings of Jesus and the latter sections of the New Testament epistles are largely occupied with moral exhortations. It may be shocking to the strict evangelical but there appears to be much more space given in the Bible to counsels for practical living than to what is admittedly of greatest importance, the fact that Christ died for our sins. I am more

---

[1] E. McDonagh: *Invitation and Response* (Dublin, 1972), p. 72.

and more convinced that many Christian people who find Paul's magnificent theological statements in Romans and other epistles 'hard to understand' and mistake the call to faith as a call to believe these difficult doctrines, none the less often make a genuine response to what God did for them in Christ, by trying to do the kind thing to their neighbours and helping in good causes. Our Roman brethren may help us here, not by thinking of good works as in any way justifying, but by their realisation that the response of good works does have a place alongside the response of faith.

It is fashionable today to regard any general rule for the good life as authoritarian, legalistic, heteronomous, puritan, moralistic, rigoristic, and so thoroughly unchristian, and some moralists are at tremendous pains to demonstrate where in particular circumstances one or other of the ten commandments ought to be disobeyed. There is no doubt that there are exceptional cases, and Christian thinkers have generally realised the need of a quality called *epieikeia* (which Matthew Arnold translated as 'sweet reasonableness') in the application of moral rules. The fact remains that apart from rather unusual situations which most of us may never face, the ten commandments and other traditional Christian norms, like the fulfilling of promises, the keeping of secrets, the endurance of injuries without retaliation and abstinence from sexual intercourse outside marriage are reasonably safe guides in the practical business of living even in the late twentieth century.

The challenge of our new freedom is not so much a challenge to reject well-tried moral counsels as a challenge to discover new demands. Some of these are implicit in the Christian tradition, but have never been worked out; the Christian reaction to slavery became practical politics only at the beginning of the nineteenth century, and some of us believe that in a nuclear age the time has come to bring our Lord's teaching on non-resistance into rules for practical action.

Other new demands spring from the new situations of today, and this is perhaps one element of truth in 'situation ethics'. This applies most of all to every-day living, the common relationships of home and work and community. Here loving may often seem limited to expressions that have lost their charm, because they are so much the conventional things to do,—the giving of birthday presents, the sending of Christmas cards, the returning of hospitality or the putting of a coin in the flag-day collecting box and the like. No doubt these things are good, if sometimes a little dull, and I for one should not wish to see them abandoned. Yet genuine love should surely at times find expression in doing something new for those we love, even although it might be thought unconventional and even not quite respectable. It has been my experience in life that when I have obeyed a generous impulse, (which may well have been the guidance of the Holy Spirit), such as speaking to a stranger or sending a gift to someone who might be in need, I have indeed been moved by Christian love. When I have far too often neglected such impulses as silly or self-advertising, I have generally regretted it later.

What are puzzling today are the situations where individual action seems almost useless, and yet in which the Christian sees evils more far-reaching even than murder or theft, which need to be set right. The growing inequality between the rich who are getting richer and the poor who are getting poorer is such a wrong. The man whose income is little above the national average may salve his conscience by giving generous donations to such charities as 'War on Want', and even by welcoming increased taxation to meet social needs, but his individual action does only a very little to mitigate, and nothing to remove, the crying evil. That would require an economic and political revolution, and I think that from our past experience in Britain the revolution would not need to be a bloody one. Until Christian thinkers use their brains and then put political pressure on the government to bring about the changes needed for a more just distribution of goods, I do not think that the ordinary man is likely to pay much attention to the excellent moral counsels to individuals that Christian preachers are so ready to give. Revolutionary thinking and action is needed not only for the redistribution of wealth, but also for the banning of atomic weapons and of war generally, for the removal of the pollution brought about by an industrial urban civilisation and so on, and so on. We should not minimise what each of us can do about these things in our own small corner. That is important as a tiny contribution both to the general good and to our own moral integrity. Yet these evils are only to be lessened and abolished by large-scale political action, and this means Christian people getting together and doing something about them. At the end of the twentieth century if there are no politics in the pulpit, it looks as if there would be no morality or only a desiccated hypocritical morality in the pulpit. In recent years few of us in the Church have had the knowledge or courage to speak out against the lower taxes demanded from the very rich, which have widened the gap between rich and poor, or against those strikes which, however just in themselves, have caused unnecessary suffering to innocent and needy people. Such things can be as evil in themselves and in their consequences as acts of petty theft and thoughtless cruelty which most of us are ready to condemn.

One of the causes of this horrid situation is that while Christians generally and many unbelievers as well have accepted our Lord's teaching about love as at least something worth aiming at, we have not accepted his teaching about self-denial. The command to deny one's self occurs in the synoptic gospels more frequently than the command to love. It is not a command to do without what is necessary, or even without luxuries, as it has often been interpreted, although there is a place for asceticism and even abstinence in some situations of our Christian life. It is rather the putting of the self aside, treating one's self as of no importance, and choosing an advantage to others rather than an advantage to one's self. One reason that we so often ignore this challenge is that self-denial is a practice and outlook on life that we cannot achieve by our own efforts. Indeed the more we strive to deny ourselves the more we shall find self taking a large place in our thoughts and aspirations. A measure of self-denial can certainly be achieved by concentrating on activities which help other people, and do not affect our own interests. Yet I believe that to set oneself aside in any thorough fashion is possible only for the man who can say with Paul, 'Not I, but Christ in me'—a condition which few even of the saints have achieved in this life, but one which all humble souls may attain in the fuller life for which this life is a preparation.

One of the things that militates against self-denial of this kind is the emphasis that has been placed on merit in conventional theology—Christ's merits if not our own. I am not denying for a moment that there is a tendency for good actions to have in the long run good consequences and for bad actions to have bad consequences. It is of such consequences that the New Testament is speaking when it talks of rewards, and our common experience confirms the truth of this teaching. Yet we are on very slippery ground if we say that we deserve these rewards. Modern psychology is probably right in emphasising our heredity and our environment as at least in part the determinants of our actions, and for neither of these can we be held responsible. And here the psychologists may not be far from those theologians who have affirmed that all that is good in us depends on the grace of God. It remains to me a theological problem why we should be regarded as responsible for our wrongdoing, but not at all for our right doing. We shall probably never know how far we are free to choose, but our very ignorance makes at least two moral demands on us—never to judge others, and never to pride ourselves on our own accomplishments. It would, I believe be truer to the mind of Christ, and incidentally helpful to the reunion of Catholics and Protestants if the word 'merit' and its equivalents were to disappear from our theological vocabulary.

When we use the words 'morals' and 'immorality' in common speech we are commonly thinking of sexual morals and sexual immorality, and it is a fact of history that Christian moralists in the past have too often been obsessed with sexual sins. Unfortunately the same obsession, although differently directed, is common to all mankind—hence the prominence of sex on the television and cinema screens. We explain this without shame today by saying that sexual desire is universal and natural, and of course this is true. Perhaps it is just another way of putting this to say that sex is something we share with the animal world, and so it is possible to engage in and enjoy sexual activities at a purely animal level. Those who do so, and I suspect there may be many, are fulfilling a biological function but they are not being true to their dignity as human beings made in the image of God, male and female. The mistake that the Church has at times made in an ascetic attitude to sex and an exaltation of virginity and celibacy was a failure to realise that sex need not remain at the animal level, but like other elements in our nature, can be developed into a relationship, involving not only the physical aspects which will still be there, but man's highest spiritual aspirations, and most of all, the capacity of selfless love. Self-denial in the sexual relationship does not mean abstinence from sexual relations, but the giving of the self to the other for the sake of the other as a much misunderstood Paul suggested (I Cor. 7: 3–5). Christians should by counsel and example demonstrate this positive attitude to sex, that marriage can be truly 'marriage in the Lord'. At the same time they must realise, as some of us can do from our own experience, that in the sphere of sexuality there are factors which can lead to the temporary or even the permanent collapse of a good and happy life. To those in such a situation the Christian must be ready to offer understanding and fellowship.

CHAPTER TEN

Prospice!

When I was a teenager, I was exceedingly shocked to hear my father say in a sermon that the teaching of the Bible was that the powers of good and of evil would continue in conflict until the end of the world. My youthful idealism had cherished the dream of a steadily increasing victory of the forces of good, the kind of progress that Tennyson depicted in his poem, 'Locksley Hall', which I greatly admired at the time. Any other possibility seemed to me an almost blasphemous questioning of the good purpose of God for his universe. Part of my mind still clings to a hope of this kind, although I admit that the biblical grounds for it are rather flimsy, and there has been much in the last half-century to shake one's faith in inevitable progress—nuclear destruction, the pollution due to what are assumed to be technological advances, and the increase of crime in spite of great developments in secular education guided by the latest psychological expertise. There has in the course of history been progress in certain limited spheres. The abolition of slavery in its conventional form was a real step forward to a better world, and I have good hope that war in its familiar form may be similarly abandoned as a way of settling international disputes. There is, however, much to suggest that new evils will appear to replace old ones. This certainly seems to be the lesson of the American prohibition experiment, attempted in high idealism, but productive of more evils than it cured.

Of one thing I feel sure. The struggle against evil, whether it be that of the individual personally resisting temptation or that of the community trying to remove a public wrong, gets real significance from the Christian view that this life is a preparation for the life of eternity. If this universe is in any sense what Keats called 'the vale of soul-making', the hard discipline involved in our human efforts both to be better men individually and to make our world a better world may be the necessary means to accomplish this. Only I should like to think of it not as the best way of making 'souls', which appear to be rather shadowy abstractions, but the best way of preparing full-blooded persons for a new life of fellowship and joy. In our customary Christian language the best preparation for the life of heaven is to try to make this present world as like to the heaven we aspire to as we can. This of course is not the whole story. We do want our children, and the succeeding generations, to grow up in the kind of world where they will be able to live lives that are good in every way. That is certainly not the world of materialistic hedonism, the kind of heaven on earth that is glorified by the mass media today.

Yet, however much I desire to see this world a better and happier place, I am now more inclined to accept my father's more pessimistic teaching, provided it is supplemented, (as I am sure it was in his case), by a belief in the second coming of our Lord. And, while including this belief in the Christian faith I confess, let me dissociate myself again from the many cranks who have calculated the date of this event and have held that the predictions of Scripture are to be literally fulfilled. I do not believe that those who are alive at the time of the second coming will meet the Lord in the air, as if they were parachuting in reverse. Indeed it may be that we have a clear indication as to how biblical predictions in this matter may be fulfilled from the manner in which Old Testament prophecies were fulfilled at the first coming of the Messiah. Certainly some of these predictions showed extraordinary foresight—witness the 53rd chapter of Isaiah, but by and large they were not fulfilled in the way that biblical scholars of that time expected. Again the historical fact that first-century Christians expected the immediate return of Christ and that this hope was disappointed should warn us, as our Lord himself did, that we have no knowledge of the date of this event. Incidentally the realisation that their hopes of an immediate return were disappointed does not seem to have weakened to any degree the faith and hope of the early Christians. To put it in a more secular way, I do not believe that the consummation of God's purpose for the human race on this planet is to be accomplished by human endeavour, however Christlike, although human endeavours may have a subsidiary part to play, for example, in preaching the gospel to all nations (Matt. 24: 14). This consummation requires divine action, perhaps in some respects analogous to what happened in Palestine in the first century of our era. The glory of the second coming may not be displayed in the celestial fireworks which some literalists have expected; it is much more likely to resemble that glory which men of insight saw in the Word made flesh in the life and death of Jesus. There seems to me to be little hope of the transformed universe all good men would like to see, unless there is some such divine intervention.

I imagine that a statistician who accepted the orthodox Christian teaching of a parousia or second coming, would, none the less, in view of its not having happened during the last two thousand years, reckon the probability of its happening during my lifetime as very low, and, in some ways I feel sorry for this. On the other hand this statistician would certainly reckon the probability of my dying within the next few years as very high. Every older Christian must come to terms with the fact that, apart from the contingency of a twentieth-century parousia, he is going to die. At first sight the right reaction for a Christian would appear to be sheer joy at the thought of departing into the nearer presence of Christ, and taking one critical step forward to joys that are beyond words to express. It is not, however, as simple as that. We are passing out into the unknown, whether to an intermediate state or to our final destiny, about which the language of Scripture is certainly figurative and often seems ambiguous. There is a natural dread of the unknown, something that a man experiences when he has to change his occupation and environment even during this life, and, apart from the assurance of Christ's companionship, the world beyond may look a very strange world. There are teachings of Paul which indicate that he anticipated a day of judgment for believers as well as unbelievers (I Cor. 3: 13–15), and this judgment does not always seem to be one of vindication. There is a natural sorrow at parting for a time from friends, a sorrow with which Jesus showed sympathy at the grave of Lazarus. (The idea that Jesus wept in grief over his followers' lack of faith on that occasion would suggest to me a Jesus lacking in human understanding.) My attitude to death at my best moments is not one of triumphal welcome, which I do not find even in Paul, but rather one of quiet confidence that the goodness and mercy which have followed me all the days of my life will still be with me and ensure that I shall have a place in my Father's house for ever. And, although sometimes this confidence has wavered when my thoughts have not been directed to Christ, at other times it has been a real comfort and strength as friends have passed into the unseen world. The quiet confidence of a Christian funeral is in happy contrast to the ostentatious displays of grief in which pagans sometimes indulge.

'It is appointed for men to die once, and after that comes judgment' (Heb. 9: 27). While it may be that the writers of the New Testament sometimes use the language of Jewish legalism in a way that is misleading to us, there can be no doubt that the reality of judgment in some sense is an integral part of the Christian gospel. As I have already suggested in my fifth chapter, the more painful facts of human history and of personal experience do indicate that one tendency at work in this mysterious universe is that evil-doing brings unhappy consequences. This is expressed in the Hindu doctrine of karma as well as in Paul's solemn assertion that 'whatever a man sows that he will also reap' (Gal. 6: 7). There are of course considerations which qualify the figurative language with which Scripture pictures this judgment in terms of an oriental judge's court. The fourth gospel suggests that this judgment is going on all the time, for when a man's life is seen in the light of Christ's holiness, it is automatically (in a very mixed metaphor!) weighed in the balance and found wanting. 'This is the judgment, that the light has come into the world, and men loved darkness rather than light, because their deeds were evil' (John 3: 19). If the experience of death is, as Paul suggests, an experience of coming into the more immediate presence of Christ, it must mean a more decisive experience of this kind of judgment. Again, and here we are right in the older tradition, for the believer the last judgment must be a judgment of vindication, for it is part of our faith that Christ won such vindication for us on the cross, however little we understand it. Yet, as I have already suggested, even for the man who has put his faith in Christ, and shared in the work of his Church, the fire of judgment may burn up his work, although 'he himself will be saved, but only as through fire' (I Cor. 3: 15). It is certain that God will bring good out of evil not merely in the sad mischances of our present life but out of what we sometimes label unscripturally and inaccurately as eternal punishment. I have shared at times the soft view of my generation that even our limited understanding of the love of God in Christ makes it impossible for us to accept the traditional Christian teachings about judgment and hell. Yet just as it is impossible to deny that there are what seem cruelly hard experiences to face in this life, it may well be that for some at any rate there is need of a hard discipline beyond the grave. We should probably think of it in terms of treatment in a psychiatric hospital rather than in terms of the torments of the traditional purgatory. The love of God may demand such a further discipline. I do not know!

I have been tempted to speculate as to what happens after death to those who have never heard the gospel message and those who have rejected it, many from sheer indifference, but some with an honest determination to face the facts. I do not believe that the teaching of the New Testament helps us to answer such questions, except to tell us of a God who deals in love and mercy with all men, even with those who reject his love. Much of what I have written in this chapter is based on what at best are probable inferences. None the less I am confident that after passing through the gate of death I shall have the same trust in the God revealed in Christ as I have had in my best moments here. Christ did something so wonderful in his cross and resurrection that death and judgment and hell have now very little terror. What I now see through a glass very dimly, I shall then see face to face, and Jesus Christ who died for me will be the focal point of that vision.

Epilogue

A weakness in writing a confession of faith in the evening of a man's life is that he concentrates on those aspects of his life which he has been taught to regard as specifically religious. For a Christian this means concentration on one's response to Jesus Christ. While I know that he should have had the dominating and controlling place in my own life, I must admit that life has had for me joys and interests which have not been fully integrated into my Christian faith. There are human experiences that have meant a great deal to me—the good companionship in the narrower circle of the home, and in wider relationships, sometimes with non-believers, the high adventure of trying to discover the truth in small matters as well as large, the enjoyment of natural scenery particularly in the hills, and of colour in art, the amusement provided by the eccentricities of University dons and others with, I hope, a side-glance at my own, the charm of little children even at their naughtiest and the simple enjoyment of food and drink. All these and many other things are good gifts of God to his children, and if my interest in them has sometimes taken precedence over interest in my own salvation (an interest which may become dangerously self-centred) and in the welfare and salvation of others, I trust I shall be forgiven. There are things that I regret. Music, except in colourful ballet, and participation in games either as spectator or as player, have meant almost nothing to me, although they clearly play so great a part in the lives of most people in my generation. What I regret more is that I have not, except rarely, been conscious of the presence and interest of Christ in my more mundane pursuits.

For he is the one that really matters. As I grow older, a great many religious interests, about which at one time I felt strongly, are now less important to me, and I am inclined to view arguments about them with a little humour, if not with a more derogatory attitude. Am I a Calvinist, as I certainly once was in my theological thinking, or an Arminian? What, or rather who, should, I am sure, mean more to me is the Christ made known to me almost exclusively in the Bible, but in teaching there that has been generally confirmed by my experience of life. So I would end this little book with a quotation from Myers' *Saint Paul*, which expresses my aspiration rather than my achievement, and one that was very dear to my partner in life:

> Yea, thro' life, death, thro' sorrow and thro' sinning
>   He shall suffice me, for he hath sufficed:
> Christ is the end, for Christ is the beginning,
>   Christ the beginning, for the end is Christ.

www.ingramcontent.com/pod-product-compliance
Lightning Source LLC
Chambersburg PA
CBHW051957290426
44110CB00015B/2275